These dancers She leaps up. ..... catches her.

Working Better

These workers want to make something new. They listen to each other's ideas. Now they will have a better plan.

Working Together

by Elena Martin

Table of Contents

Consultant: Dwight Herold, Ed.D., Past President, Iowa Council for the Social Studies

Working Faster

Working together can mean work gets done faster.

Cleaning up all these leaves is a big job. It's a good thing this girl has help!

Building a car is a big job.
More workers will help the
job get done faster.

Some jobs are very, very big!
It takes many workers to get
the job done.

Working More Safely

Working together can mean work gets done more safely.

One firefighter holds the ladder. That makes it safer for others to climb up.

Divers always dive with a buddy. The buddy can help out if there is trouble.

Who is the leader here? How does he help the class work better?

Working as a Family

A family works together.
Everyone helps out. This girl
is helping her mom cook.

Each member of this band does something different. One person is the leader. Having a leader makes the music sound better.

The coach is the leader of this team. How does a coach help a team play better?

This boy and his mom work together in the garden.

Working together can be fun!